Compass Head

Nat Hall

NORDLAND

www.nordlandpublishing.com

Copyright

Published by Nordland Publishing 2016

ISBN E-book: 978-82-8331-013-9
ISBN Print: 978-82-8331-014-6

Dedication

For three generations of mothers,

Mémée Duval, my great grandmother,

Mamie, my grandmother

and my mother.

Contents

INNER SPACE

SEASONS

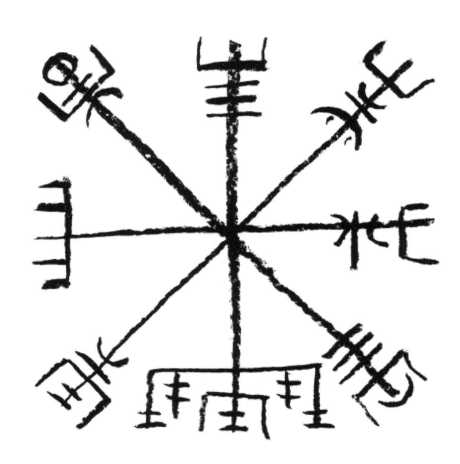

Foreword
The Meaning of North

One beach, one wish, one little girl who dreamt of crossing seas to find new land beyond the horizon.

Nor: *Nor*man – *Nor*se. One syllable, a saga that defines heritage & life. In this book, I take an epic journey through time, seas, shores and headlands to find at last my home as a woman and a poet. I explore the sky, the sea and landscapes through my geopoetical journey, but also my innerscapes— those imaginary places in Shetland and across the globe; Japan, Native America and the Norse (or "Viking") worlds, where I turn into the *immobile* traveller.

The concept of *Geopoetics,* the brainchild of Glasgow-born & Brittany-based writer Kenneth White, has always been central to my poetry. To be at one with and in tune with the *open world* and its riches. I feel very much part of such a world. It remains the celebration of my shore, whether Norman or Scottish.

Compass Head embraces the journey from my native Normandy (Land of the Northmen) to 60°N and the Shetland isles, via a short incursion in Provence. Along the way, I marked my passage with stones. Like beacons, they show the way. If there's a duality to my tongue, this is because my northern roots have flourished across the currents of the North Sea.

And if you travel to 60°N, and make your way to the tip of Shetland's main island, just behind Robert Stevenson's lighthouse, you will find Compass Head, and perhaps you will find me too.

Nat Hall, Shetland Isles, 2016

1

"Compass Skull"

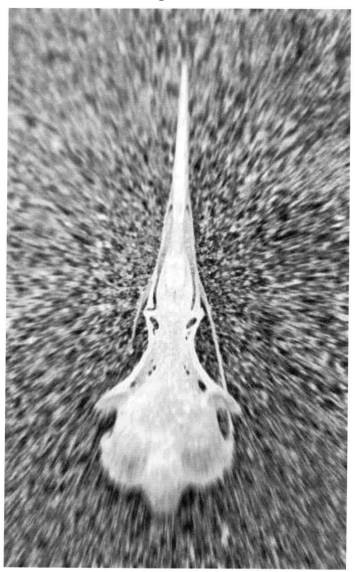

Connections

"No one knows our universe is unique. Flip it, and be prepared to hear it speak."

E. Morgan

(Universes)

The Chemist's Lab

It all started elemental, a single H – God's creation.
Clashing atoms created light;
look for white clouds
in this emptiness
we call space –
cosmic coldness,
his perfection.

> Beyond the belt of loneliness,
> two atoms fused to make a star;
> it's shining there brighter than white
> behind the red of nebulae
> like a lone ghost,
> or an angel.

Magnetic fields,
cosmic cobwebs, I trapped debris & solar flares
like butterflies inside a net;
a *home in space* for a mortal,
the turning earth... the growing moon...
the visionary rendezvous.

Skydiver

"We have increasingly become phantoms.
... To Jupiter to Hell and any place..."

I look at you from out of space,
I see great rifts, long mountain chains,
cyclonic eyes steamed up with rain,
white against blue.

I need to delve in that membrane
that protects you –
I might burn through your stratosphere,
my heart feels like a meteor.
Gravity retracts all my fears.
I look a spider in your sky –
I'm still looking for your garden,
stretch of heather you call Eden,
let me open my parachute.

It's like a dream,
        strangest of game –
        I braved your shield to hear your song,
            I dared to dive,
        I still have stardust on my suit.

La presse à pommes

Parfum de brume
dans le pré,
mille gouttes d'eau,
filles de rosée,
je vois encore ces vieux pommiers,
fruit de l'enfance acidulé,
cueilli au premier jour d'automne -
ma Normandie,
ce doux verger, prend
des allures
vert monochrome.
Octobre baptise les toits d'ardoise de la Cité,
mes petits pieds sur les pavés
entre les flaques
sautillent et dansent -
une main tendre pour me guider,
fruit de l'amour acidulé,
je vois encore
la cour et la cabane de
ma petite enfance,
haricots en bouquets sous
la tôle ondulée,
Papi sourire,
    la presse à pommes.

A Papi et Mamie, mes grands parents bien aimés

6

The Apple Press

Perfume of fog
in our meadow, a thousand drops –
daughters of dew,
I still recall old apple trees,
fruit of my acidulated
childhood,
I picked you up on
autumn day –
my Normandy, this
soft orchard,
takes many forms
in monochromic green.
October has christened
the slate roofs of our homes;
my childish feet just hop and dance
between puddles on
paving stones –
a tender hand to guide
my life;
fruit of acidulated love,
I still remember
this courtyard
of my early childhood,
beans in bouquets,
my old sandpit...
Papi smiling,
    the apple press.

For Papi and Marie, my beloved grandparents

A Haiku

Outward -

out, in your boat,

unafraid of riding wild waves, tearing sea.

#haiku fae #60N

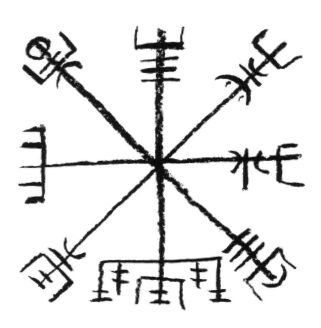

My Great Grand Mother's Hands

Let fingers time travel.
Mother prunes vine,
        grand mother knits –
there in my soul I'm still feeling
        my great grand mother's hands.
Time ties strong bones around bollards.
No more *Terre-Neuvas,* sixareens…
Lerwick,
Fécamp or Baltasound,
barrels belong to celluloid,
filed, filleted,
microcosm on microfiche
like a treasure
in B&W.
That woman gutting fish
looks like my ancestor:
head dressed in a white scarf,
Benedictine sister –
their knives so feverish
on the shore of both lands,
Norman or Shetlandic…
Silver nitrate turned to yellow,
Eyes on postcard revive
one tale of the *hareng.*

For three generations of mothers

9

Les mains

Laissez les doigts défier le temps.

Ceux de ma mère taillent la vigne,
ceux de sa mère, le calico -
petites mains,
mains ouvrières...
là, dans mon âme,
les mains de mon arrière grand mère,
maintes fois meurtries par la mer,
le temps amarre les destinées
le long des quais.
Lerwick,
Fécamp ou Baltasound,
plus de Terre-Neuvas, sixareens...
Les tonneaux brillent sur
pellicule, fichés,
filletés,
un microcosme sur microfiche,
comme un trésor en
noir et blanc.
Cette femme qui vide le poisson calque
les traits de mon ancêtre:
menue, coiffée d'un
foulard blanc,
petite soeur bénédictine -
lame normande ou shetlandaise,

mains écorchées en parallèle des
deux côtés de l'océan.
Trésor de nitrate d'argent écaillé de jaune par le temps,
anime mon coeur, ce loup de mer – défie
mes doigts, ceux de leurs mères,
ravive l'épopée du hareng.

Pour trois générations de mères

Errances

Au fil de l'onde et des
rivages,
les pas se fondent
entre galets
et sable
blanc;
que des bras de mer
ensorcellent
pour se noyer dans l'océan.

L'enfant mémorise la terre,
cornets de glace et cerf-
volants,
d' Etretat
aux Saintes-Maries-de-la-
Mer,
vagues encablures
du temps...

Au gré des arches & des
falaises,
depuis l'Aiguille,
craie ou Crin Blanc -
les mares sâlent le
caractère,
ton c?ur si fier bat en gitan.
Nomade en quête de
déserts,
Tu erres dans les couloirs du
vent,
Nord par Nord-Ouest,
Là où le goémon
emplit l'air
de tous tes rêves
d'adolescent.

Wanderings

From coast to coast,
footprints blend
between pebbles and
white
sand;
bewitched by Sounds
To drown inside the ocean
world.

Child's mind imprints sense
of the earth,
ice cones and kites,
from Etretat
to Les Saintes-Maries-de-la-
Mer,
time's own
stone's throws...

Along cliffs and arches,
from the Aiguille*,
chalk or Crin Blanc* -
tides add salt to your
character,
outside the cage, proud
gypsy heart.
Nomad in search of empty
space,
you roam in the wind's
corridors
North by North-West,
where wrack
fills air
from all your adolescent's
dreams.

12

De ces montagnes de galets,
Dieppe - Dungeness,
tu as l'étoffe des géants;

écoute les rumeurs de la Manche,
dans ses humeurs,
tu vagabondes hors réverbères,
discuttes avec les goélands.

Toujours plus Nord,
là où
la lumière éphémère,
dans cet abysse de l'hiver
attise les bas-fonds de la mer;
à pleins poumons, sans amertume,
sur le sable, les filins d'écume,
relient Mallaig à St Ninian.

A chaque grand banc ou bout de terre,
Les poches gonfflées de coquillages,
ton coeur, siléger, virevoltant entre hier & maintenant;

rappelle-toi,
le chant du monde dans les galets
du bocage saxon ou normand,
ce littoral

From those great mountains of shingle,
Dieppe – Dungeness,
you have the makings of giants;

hear the Channel's waves of gossip,
in its array of marine moods,
you wander off lit beaten tracks,
argue your case with herring gulls.

Always more north,
here, where
thin light ephemeral
inside this abyss of winter
rekindles dreams from the seabed;
with all their strength, so bitterless,
threads of white lace
Connect Mallaig to Ninian's Sands.

To each grand bank or tongue of land,
with equal pockets full of shells,
your flitting heart
in between yesterday & now,

remember, child -
song from the earth inside shingle
on either side of The Channel –
Saxon, Norman;
this littoral,

13

remonté à contre-courant,
dessine toutes tes nuits
boréales,
Sandwick,
cartographié
dans chaque étoile,
a esquissé ton univers,
vert-orangé de l'atmosphère.

Ton coeur a trouvé son élan.

where you wandered against the
grain,
helped you etch all boreal nights
Sandwick,
cartographed
inside every star,
drafted and spelled your
universe,
in atmospheric hues of green.

Your heart has found its
impetus.

"Bonxies in flight"

Confession to a Foreigner

Look left and right,
stay still or sigh.
Who chooses one's parents
or that side of pavement
to learn to walk?
Glasgow,
Gisors or Soweto,
we were all born
inside a planetary square –
and had to grow
where we were told.
Born somewhere.
I toddled on a cobbled road
double-banded in yellow lines.
Pedestrian turned to driver,
destiny swirls at roundabouts.
Like you I keep to the left side,
trying to blend in the traffic;
forget my roots,
they're just like yours –
Guillaume,
William
jumbled up in a cul-de-sac,
quelle différence?
I had to start and turn somewhere.

Twangs in my tongue
might make you smile,
forgive my nationality!

I was born somewhere.
Me laisser ce repère, ou perdre la boussole.

Boat to Wonderland

To let it slip, to let it slip,
she loved you more for it

You set me free, there on that boat to Wonderland.

Shambolic sea or greener grass,
We look away and gain
control.

You didn't really mean to hurt –
you held me tight against blue sky,
a torn ticket to Wonderland.

Wrapped in woollen,
we brace ourselves to brave sea breeze;
south-easterlies to Wonderland,

sea-spray, solace,
you look solemn beyond my eyes,
this camera.

I'm still feeling strength in your arms,
will to believe in Wonderland.

You want us close,
still on that deck among cold crowd –
immortalised in our present.

Life Whispers

The ocean breath tells us a tale.

Waves in the air,
 waves on the sea,
  awakes senses -

there I hear seals dreaming,
seabirds talk in their
sleep,
 whales
 whisper to us on surface
   that they found love in
  plankton bloom;
against rocks
 wild anemones
  open their arms,
dance in rock pools.

Around one
  world,
   a symphony
told to sailors by
you, fair
 winds.

Where on Earth?

In between salt and *selkies'* caves,
    where basalt stands taller than waves -

north of bird rock,
    everlasting celestial clock.

In between blood & horizon,
    where sailors seem to lose reason;

north of beyond,
    as nightmares sound so moribund...

And beyond that, salt-bird-rock-blood and horizon.

Where would we find what we look for?
What do we seek? What,
Where?

    Where on Earth?

Are we there yet?
Have lost my way, fisherman's net.

"Sumburgh Lighthouse" (detail)

Tower of Light

On her high heels, this old lady,
between sky, salt & Atlantic,
watches each
day
like a
bridesmaid.
your fog horn, now revamped in red,
your husky voice,
ephemeral.

    Sullied by spray,
        you defy the Roost in anger;
   salt so futile in tidal time,
you stay mistress of your
headland.
               Destined to tame wildest of waves, you've
                          never shun for
                          ghost pirates,
             but awoke dreams inside one child,
                   one secret world,
                       elemental.
Like a treasure,
your silhouette unites dreamers in brotherhood,
   friend of black backs, you have seduced our universe.
All around you, loyal fulmars won't mourn summer,
they twist & slide in their hundreds...
Solitary yet immortal,
   your spirit beams around
      the clock.

Hame

«Today you see far down a
mountainside,

out over islands to a sure horizon.»

C. De Luca

(Journeys)

A Tale of Two Harbours

You need to look at a compass,
each arrow points out to a sea;
through a fisheye,
an ocean –
a tongue of land
where we can read
a world of men,
fishers, crofters, navigators,
wave wanderers;
in search of life
on greener shores...
They swapped a sail
for a few oars,
scout ravens flew out
to new cliffs;
they pulled their boats and kissed
the ground,
built a new home,
hope & beliefs.
Today
we still dig in the sand,
unearth our past,
look through
the sea,
where mother
wind once blew their sail,
always westwards,
as if to flee.

Landmarks

What's an island?
Top of invisible mountain
an ocean submerged,
as if to cut bridges
for those
who
dreamt
of boats inside
a shed - shreds of
oak beams for a transom...

What's an island?
The gentle green of rounded heads,
fashioned by ice, wind, elements;
elemental as emeralds
found on the edge
of ocean lore...

What's an island?
A blanket of peat on a rock,
home for a snipe or
a redshank -
where
folk
gather in
in preparation for winter.
What's an island?
a grassy slope off a cliff edge
where we come to sit
in the fog to hear
the world,
long
languid

lament of curlews,
lone rain goose calling
for his love.

What's an island?
The starting point on sailors' chart,
crowned by a dream of
a lighthouse,
home,
as they
stravaig on
oceans they never
thought would have a shore
with whiter sand.

What's *your* island?
A bit of green kept so secret,
wilderness grows like marram grass
in sand so sensitive to wind,
sea rockets thrive
in primal sun?

Let pebbles wander off wet sand.

"Waterline"

The Oared Folk

They're rowing,
curved silhouettes towards fringe of one horizon

they're rowing,
out to ocean they dream to tame

they're rowing,
oar against kabe, same humli-baand

they're rowing,
palms against wood create friction

they're rowing,
clockwork bodies, mechanical

away from all familiar craigs,
elliptic bays,
light selkies songs –

temptation fae da waterhorse

they're rowing
and I watch you

barefoot in
sand.

Dis Midder Tongue

Fae native lands,
Faroe,
Scotland,
Cornwall, Ireland –
Brittany or
Provence...
Wir midder tongue
lives in our souls –
du cannot die!
...We didn't
choose words and
grammar – but
heard whispers deep
in *wir midder's womb*
dis midder tongue,
spoken by folk,
so familiar –
you are a gem,
not just
that organic fruit
acidulated
through
voices, accents
and time.

To me,
enlightened
sooth moother, du
sounds juist as boannie as mine –
dis midder tongue
I heard whispered.
My heart is open
ta dy wirds -vowels
an sounds (!)
I welcome *dee*
with open arms –
...To breathe
laek dee,
I need *ta ken*
dis mechanics –
...just adopt me as
dy new bairn!

Ninian Song

1.

Listen to this
shore

Gone half past five,
rollers talk clear in unison against shelled sand,
with hooded crows as parliament and jet-lagged
light on Atlantic...

2.

Modern Pilgrims

They come to meet with
an island,
heads against sun,
feet against
sand,
wander across synchronised waves,
all around them, whizzing
shadows on
white
shoreline,

they tread like
saints against skyline,
insignificants to
turnstones, in
tête-à-tête with NE wind.
And when you look from Earth distance,
their hearts travel at
speed of
clouds.

"Modern Pilgrims"

Homeworld

60 to the highest dreamer!
I look at Earth, ancient part of
your American universe -
domes of heather,
above ocean
our Atlantic;
clear,
honey,
crimson,
tungsten sky,
    mire, meadow, multicolour,
        majestic shades of viridian,
           where birdsong loops like luggage left
on
                carousels...
        Where peat fills air
        through chimney
    stacks,
like rising smoke
from tanned
tepees;
where each geo sounds like a shelter to
    fishermen,
        where you can feel
           bright hearts moving.

Bird on your Shoulder

So many feathers inside cage.
Long, black, broken,
creased keratin,
inside my book of elements,
jinxes and spells,
blend in
    swift's tongue with
        snapdragon and asphodel -
            tell me you can dream on the wing,
      share an apple with a waxwing,
    high on a roof with
a blackbird.

Chose si belle,

    above spring waves with storm petrels,
      that avian urge to
    reach your home, and
loose your way across
    the sea.

Hay's Dock

Come to the wharf at 5 o'clock.

In between chunks of mango fruit you bought in haste at
the Co-op,
tirricks swoop free among voices
that tell us from
another
time.
Strange
choral through
four megaphones,
where children sing to a piano,
whilst Tammie speaks of his croft world
and Edna yarn about her past life in Glasgow...
So many stories recorded for the benefit of the wind,
the herring gull and passer-by,
where Maggie's ghost makes folk listen to
one dark tale of the island.

Sea Rockets

There we walk,
bare footed, deep in sand -
crystallised souls
before
each tide,
emerald-green,
adrift in spray,
afraid to fray...
Mystical scent awakes
our dream,
invisible,
pinkish-lilac,
fresh,
succulent.
Wave after wave,
sea rockets
have
womanly charms,
so innocent.
They dance alone, reel in
light breeze;
firmly rooted,
    like us,
        in sand.

Home

a festival of scented peat

smouldering low at a slow pace –

a bit of love

when all is dark.

Pirates de l'Air (Fish Hijackers)

Out, on Midfield,

a nest,

Mousa's bathing -

sunshine,

selkies, in East Pool rest;

Common Mouse-ear, the
waterline.

Where storm petrels headed

North-West,

broch and daeks nurse many
offspring;

up on Midfield, frantic

unrest:

known silhouettes of chestnut
wings!

Above heather,

    sheer battlefield:

solan, tirricks -

sole game of death, wild
piracy.

These fish robbers,

proud and shameless!

But above all,

clear signature of

the bonxie.

Sushi in Hamnavoe

She, Sakura Shinguji, savours sushi
by the seashore –
Shetlandic taste, in *sho-yu* sauce...
Fish, rice rouléed,
seaweedy spell –
laced like otters in
sugar kelp...

Sâlé-sacré, sâlé-Sake.

Play-transforming into Highness,
her silky robe
doesn't hide smiles,
cherry blossoms
at Altaness –
her soul & heart in parallel,
20 degrees north off
Tokyo.
She, so refined & delicate.
Artist at heart,
she loves colours,
washed through water or in
her plate –
her life runs free,
framed on white walls through
the chambers of her castle,
guarded by gods black as ravens...
No earthquake bird will change her mind,
                                    all is quiet in Hamnavoe.

Keep Zen

Water-wind-waltz.

Empty your heart from all its ink, dirty & dark, indelible. Let one by one flow down your thoughts – that rationale that plays a trick in the meanders of your soul. Today all junk wrecked in my head feels like driftwood lost on a beach, eaten away by time and salt. There's a blue rope tied to a buoy, orange in colour, platonic. It stares at us like a decoy. I love that word in dialect that describes life washed off by waves – Shetlanders call it *da shoormal.*

There's a heartbeat in each limpet that wants to escapes at high tide. They stick to rocks like Sellotape, until water fills in their pride... Look for their prints on this blank page; each one of them's a hedonist.

Mire-wind-rain.

Tie up your boots, we go uphill. Fishermen built a thousand meads to remind them where to find home and family...

Peaty liquid runs in my veins to irrigate our wildest streams; theatrical like a cascade, always rushing to drain our pain – elemental to quench our dreams.

Wickerlady of Lovers Loan

Wickerman dreamt on
his first night.
He, Adam-shaped out of
shy hands
on the fifth day,
begged for a bride.
Dream, dream Wickerman –
Malicious moon mirrored your wish on a lochan.
The grass grew green on his island.
God kept busy on his first week.
At Lovers Loan creator wove
perfect wicker.
He would give her
long silver hair to please the wind –
generous curves, courage,
crown, strength,
a croft to shelter from storm eyes...
her love to live each new morning –
two caddy lambs by early spring,
a lovers' song,
  her Wickerman.

"Lerwick, Old Waterfront"

Shower on the Esplanade

High tide,
low cloud over Bressay and Sound -
Victoria Pier bare to spring rain.
The Old Harbour echoes crash, crushing of
cold drops; in single file,
shags rush feathers
low above waves.
All is serene,
inert and
grey.
In between
clouds,
Lerwigians
glide against granite in
low skyline – slippery flagstones quickens pace.
A beam of light revives their smiles;
carpark keeper out of his
box peeps at
windscreens – you
can't miss him, all dressed in red.
Below my feet, pier and bollards, *tysties* paddle along our
tugs,
Jim is waiting in his taxi.
My eyes and heart back inside sun, time has run out on
my ticket – time to depart and wave goodbye to
the sea, gulls, pier and those
clouds

The Wakening

The Nothing.

The heart of God.

The coldness and silence.

The dark side of the Earth.

The disappearance of Venus.

The final thread of a nightmare.

The naked limbs on the mattress.

The shrieking plea of the *shalder*.

The way you curse the alarm clock.

The twisted guts, chaotic head...

the revenge of the alcohol.

The urge to kill a hangover.

The ray of sun behind curtains.

And smile of God,

    his forgiveness.

Northern Roost

Fly away home,
60 degrees on your atlas –
hearts get giddy
above those clouds...
serenity dazzles my eyes.
Life looks obscure
here in winter,
where pink sunsets seem
too short-lived;
my motorways roar
in the sky
with swans & geese
as sole bearings.
Flying out,
always higher to freeze
my tears;
ground is for love,
shared in our smiles,
home-grown
gardens –
I packed it all
secure, so safe,
wrapped in my soul
to deter miles,
10,000 feet.

My eyrie grows bigger
in size;
this northern roost
shelters our
wings
from
wind and
rain,
elevates
us
at each
sunrise...

Grey fuselage
will take
me
home.

Earth Giants

Tell me the story of the stone.

    Behind each rock stands a giant.

Old Man of Storr has a brother on an island North by

North east, lost in darkness most of winter,

who answers to Old Man of Hoy -

ancient headlands now

separated by a

shore;

how

do

they

grow is a

mystery only

water carves deep in time...

And if you obey your compass,

you will enter the dragon's den & face

its teeth, polished by sleek

North Atlantic & ballroom Moon

laced inside tides;

salt, satin, sari,

Nordic style.

They are immobile travellers in

the face of

    seafaring stars.

60N Song

Today I woke to silent sky.
There's nothing else to talk about,
but starlings singing
inside sun,
incessant
serenade tricksters that click like
small men in their tongue -
endless arguments
from proud
gulls,
February,
pale morning blue.

Love has no bound,
barrier or
passport -
but trails in every heart from mountains to the sea,
and flies with guillemots,
arctic terns,
kittiwakes
to reach out to headlands
only your fingers
feel...

With compass & passion.

Together

Now come undone.

Inside the garden they gathered,
in between branches and dawn's pearls, as
blue dominated their world, and blackbirds dreamt deep
in ivy.
Asleep they fell on satin leaves, as sunrise burnt their
game of lust,
entangled in jet black iris that fell to prey,
pleasure and dust.

As furtive as they may vanish,
they will nestle in
secret leaves,
feel warmth
from
an
afternoon
sun,
flutter along sweet
summer breeze, in
an orchard,
cherries
and
love.

Shipwright

No bone, just rust.

They say they nailed you on a wall,
framed inside wood,
sea drifter's
dream,
but
as
currents
took you apart,
you lost your legs as
a sailor, and
let salt
gnaw
through
your rib cage.
What's come of you defies Earth's tides,
lightless iris lost in
riptides,
your
joie de vivre
in prey to
dust...
What's left of you,
but eyes of metal on
the wall.

"shipwright"

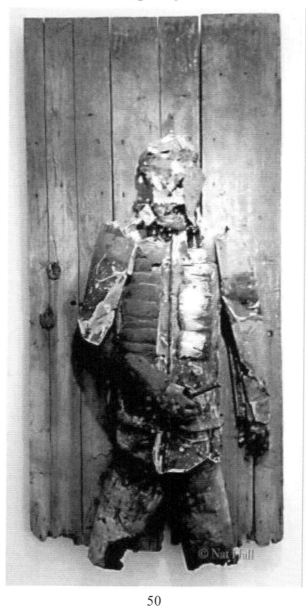

Compass Head

Now feel wingbeats of whooper swans in
    between sea
            and
            northern stars.
                    Like navigators above waves,
        they need fair winds to reach headlands -
sleek magic of magnetic field,
                    a horizon,
                        flair,
                                stamina.
They may not know of meridians, our human web we
                        imagined to find our
way across

            oceans, but that
                    compass built in their heads
will guide them home
                            through day and
                                night.

                                And
            when they reach precious
    homeground,
            I hear them
                call above my head,
                as I look
                        towards
                        the
                                lighthouse.

Inner space

«where is she?
not in the old bath
where cattle drink
from the sky's green iris.»

J. Hadfield
(where is she?)

The Samurai

Gutting a fish
is like ripping yourself apart -
sharpness on the folded metal
rakes off your coat,
flaky armour;
shiny scales,
aluminium grey,
stick up like slime
on newspaper.
Gills become lungs;
ego explored with a blind blade
through the navel -
code of honour
(kendo once laid)
my fingers tainted
by fresh blood,
I feel the hand of Samurai.

Cloning Your Cactus

Look at my theory of mind.

An A to Z of my problems
to cultivate your own garden.
How can I click A into B
when I can't see the whole picture?
To you an obvious Meccano –
to me as crystal clear as mud.
How could I break things into steps?
I'd rather crush my Rice Crispies on kitchen floor!

Prioritise... Chaotic thought.

Why don't you show me starting line?
You might attract my attention.
No *eenie - meenie - minie - moe;*
help me to take a decision.
Don't you dare leave me in limbo,
my frustration will swell inside.
Trigger, tantrum, rage & meltdown –
my volcano's in eruption.

Open your eyes.
Trying to understand my mind can feel like
cloning your cactus.

You, Little Albino Sparrow

Look at yourself among the crowd,
    you don't quite mingle with the rest.
Always on the edge of the shrubs,
in-and-out, like an intruder,
whilst your kind
feasts on
oblivion.
And
yet you
shine in your own way;
majestic crown of
snow bunting,
you stand out wherever you land -
and if you're not quite a
captain, don't you forget, you're a sparrow,
fierce, quarrelsome, original,
light years ahead of
the humdrum.
I've watched you feed hours on end, don't be afraid to
watch your ground, you have a place
among my trees.

Alone in the Gale

I, the puny, inside vortex.

My gale has so many faces,
it is the howler in blackness,
    the one that scalps the Moon and hearth –
it is the ghosts tattooed on clouds, the ones that stare,
    that unleash rain like freezing knives...
It is the voice of loneliness,
    the one that hisses among walls behind
        the seam of thick curtains;
it is the shit scared lass inside,
    the one that hides and runs away, as thunder strikes
and creates light.
It is the box I won't open,
    the one that homes he-quirky Jack,
ready to spring out like a clown;
it is the smirk of the dark page,
    the one that irks in between lines...
it is the high eye of the storm,
    the one that wanders all around and spreads
        rumours in between tiles.

And I sit there,
    tight on my chair, without a mask,
ready to open your codex,
        whilst you're waltzing anti-clockwise.

"Blackbird in a gale"

In Orbit with God

Today she sought a tête-à-tête
with the Holy without a grin of derision.
Sharing an orbit with God, all but
a no-small experience.
She looked through her cylindric glass
faceted like a spider eye,
to brightest corner of his sky –
might of his light winning over
grey stubbornness from weeping clouds.

Time to clean up and dust her past.

Final tempest grew out of breath –
too tired to play with roof tiles.
One final glance through her window
sparkled with salt,
she looked serene as she blew off
her storm lantern –
her horizon now within sight.
Alone on this corner of cliffs,
amidst bracken so desolate ravens had never dared to
nest,
last of sea-pinks turned into straw, she too
could handle this harshness, grief,
anger from an early gale –
year after year, laughter & smiles,

tears from her face...
She looked solemn outside her porch.
Each paving stone would direct her
towards her wish.

Dressed in orange, she couldn't be more visible;
God doesn't mind bright oilskins...
He's accustomed to fishermen.

She walked her desert of heather.
She found her seat on a boulder N by NW.
Morning drizzle washed off her pain.
There at her feet, worn Atlantic paid its respect.
She hailed Mary so many times –
unleashed her prayers to the wind...
a strange meeting so high above ocean level.
Somehow she wished for comet trails
to reach for her star in orbit – her compassion
so far beyond blue stratosphere,
that other side, *half of the sky.*

Her mourning life inside his hands.

She threw sea mayweed to wild waves,
she blew kisses to her loved ones.
Today the wind still speaks her name.
It's like a dream; a truth or dare.

A haiku

In sombre times,
I slash sadness with a *tushkar*.

The Erratics

Don't ask boulders what they're thinking,
watching the world from the roadside –
they're just like us,
antisocial, lone, unwanted,
grey as graphite among heathrush;
bare to gales, grief, gulls & guano,
scatterlings ditched by accident...
plugged and bulldozed against their will
by ice that thawed, deserted them
on a waste hill –
like a mother who stopped to cope,
ran out of steam,
displaced her load in random fields,
fossilised tears in the matrix.

Take a close look.

Ignorance ignites derision,
     we're not lepers or heretics –
     just out of place,
     driven by dreams, running away from erosion.
      Our bedrock's full of erratics,
        dead on moraines, sick, terminal.

Green & Split Peas

God's frozen South.

Strange rendez-vous,
I frowned at sight of ocean bird,
that wandering pink albatross – tracking device,
unorthodox.
My old man warned,
Hamish helped me to the gangway;
in our linage of seafarers, twenty quid ruled my destiny.
From peat to ice, solid by-law of survival, where
world skerries look similar & men, like clones out of
bible,
I met the *Arab & the Beast.*
Harpoon in hell below zero,
with my gunner, a Lilliputian from Glasgow,
I learnt his kind would withhold smiles till the first kill.
Earth pendulum,
where water washes over deck,
I prayed to trust my young sea legs & learnt to walk to the
galley.
There, on the floor of the storeroom, bags stand alike.
My innocence mixed oats & peas, green beans fished out
off breakfast plates -
the old steward was a wise man, his compassion became
my shield.
Boy among men,
against all odds I learnt my trade,
neither meat lumps nor single pea in my porridge.

Totem Bird

I am raven,
     jet solitaire –

messenger, bridge between two worlds;
one palpable,
the other, dream,
my psychic soars above heather.
I bring spirit, inner knowledge & often scavenge
on useless.

I am message & messenger.
I sometimes call… summon or jeer –
my presence breaks
this earth silence,
you know your future is changing.
Let me awake you,
lone dreamer.

Freedom

What is freedom but a long rope
without a knot –
fibre woven by many hands,
no single use.

The cliff hanger faced to the ledge,
clinging to rock like a spider to silk & web,
in harmony with his cordage.

Freedom,
long rope without a knot –

the fisherman safe from the net,
rigging his heart to his own boat for his greatness –
soul mounted on two solid hands
to avoid wrecking hull & fate.

Freedom, rope,
knot,

the winch man on the other end,
soul hung from five rotating blades,
in search of life inside
the storm...

Sing it again: what is freedom?

Mountain, fisher, winch or plain man, we fight fibres –
tie, untie knots from our own ropes,
compressive pain.

"Freedom"

Destitute

Now imagine an empty sea,

no bottle washed up on our shores, as if the Moon had drunk it all.

Millions of words rolled inside glass stuck in sand grains,

grit & dust of those still born clouds, as if the world had stopped to talk;

absurdity of known headlands, anchors,

beacons built around cliffs, thin blue line of our horizon –

discovery of new wastelands, ladles of *bruck* around *skerries*,

flattened forests of flawless kelp,

an ocean bed deprived of silk & eiderdown...

Desolate song of dying whales,

squabbling gulls,

fishermen sat against their hulls,

heads inside hands,

as seamanship now left to rust...

Eerie silence of rotting flesh,

miles of driftnets lost & found to eternity –

in abyssian sound of sadness,

your voice and mine too scared to scream to a dry *Ness*,

destitution found deep in salt,

the unfolding of Atlantis.

67

North

I.

feel this frantic Nordic ocean
spray flies over cliff face
our heads
like dandelion
parachutes

II.

Needle

Obsessed by a magnet

Rooted so deeply in your eyes

Towards a point invisible

Hooked like a fish on a compass

III.
more north than north
muckle flugga
rocky token for a giant or a gannet
defies your bearings where
land dives inside blueness of
oblivion

Tête-à-tête

We leave watermarks everywhere
    from the bathroom to the garden.

Prints of passage on blue lino,
    (after midnight, angels tiptoe -)

like signatures tattooed in time,
on every square,

tilted to the corner of my hearth,
where you sought solace from ambers,

reassurance instead of wrath.

Voyage to the heart of our earth,
as our eyes meet in tête-à-tête,

where our voices flow like magma –
metamorphic, molten as one,

from either side of universe,
listen for footsteps on floorboards.

Mother Sea

There's nothing new brought to the shore. The lazy tide sometimes returns empty handed. Not a sandal, or drifted wood left on the beach... Afar, sea haze, like an old shroud, obscures our world, infinity. Breakers wait for bliss in shallows to unveil anger on their path. Deserted life under my feet, ivory grains hide shells devoid of eyes and jaws. Timid lugworms race against time to gasp a bit of oxygen. Their fortresses, made with wet sand, they're terrified at sanderlings! Those small waders want to stay dry – they always seem to run away from lacy surf like rewound toys. It's in their genes, mechanical. As a headdress to the splash zone, piles of disjointed sugar kelp, cured by our star, sea breeze and spray attract a squadron of starlings. V-shaped to glide through the seasons, our tinsel birds just wish to feast.

On second sight, water unveils unusual shapes. Black dorsal fins slash gentle waves. My mind dictates a name, Orca – an illusion out of a dream. I know they flirt with the surface, to catch their breath; a furtive glimpse into my world, peeping onto sun-bathing seals... Teeth in a pod roam our oceans; they know each corner of our cliffs. To them the world swims in a cave, it's just a game of hide-and-seek! In between trees in kelp forests, I imagine a racing game where fish wander without helmets – where otters glide to harvest love and sea urchins. Starfish belong to the seabed. They're hardly lifted off their floor. They share stories with the rest of the mollusc world, each word relayed through the grapevine... Tales of horror awake their wits – AC/DC, thrills and hurting, alternative, just like currents.

In mid-summer light reigns supreme on your blueness. This gigantic mass of water, larder of life, emerald-green, allows the Moon to stay asleep whilst terns and auks fish for their young. Life still at stakes hangs in their beaks; against the clock they take the plunge. Gannets slide low above the waves. They too belong to your offspring. Black-tipped white wings cut through airstreams before head butting, eyes open, the blue of your epidermis! Shoals of sand eels face this terror. In the tumult they want to scream – save their own scales from bills and jaws... They're just small fry on the ladder, for there's always a bigger fish – a bully boy ready to sneak right from above or just below. Patchwork of joys and cruelty, nature regulates our own fate. Who said our world was paved with gold? Moby Dick dreams inside my head.

Tide after tide, lazy or simply generous, I come to sit right at your edge, hear water whisper to pebbles, as if it wished to turn a page; I'm still looking for that sandal. Dolphins leap out across your waves like grasshoppers – they're just playing with young mermaids, rubber band grace. Sometimes I wish I could join in their joyous game instead of lying on the sand... I hold my kite, this aerial apparatus might help me lift our whole spirit beyond the clouds – to me they look a barrier, something so light yet sinister, impalpable. I feel so small, here on my stone, a drop of life in this cosmos. I blend my tears with wind and rain to find solace between your arms. I need to share that with you, friend, mother of life – for all I know you are aware of my anger, sorrow and rage. I wish I could catapult them beyond the ridge of light and sound.

"Waiting for Odin"

From Shell to Sand

There's nothing new or conical,
just lines of shells
        shattered,
            sheltered,
                like shields in sand –
dented,
    dated,
      daring each tide...
        rounded,
            rattled,
                rented by time.
                        My fingers felt that final wave
                            flirting with your skin
                                in wet sand,
                        smooth as a shell
                    or golden grain –
                a silky sea,
            lace on our land
    like petticoats
        loose on your legs,
            plundering,
                            plain,
                                purer than white.
            There I found solace on the sand,
        salty,
            solemn,
                    narcotic red –
                        naked,
                            sacred,
                                sculpted by
                            tears,
                                hearts of
                            nacre.

73

Tun & Scattald

Garth,
fae da Old Norse,
an arrangement of long houses with
smoky stacks,
where farmers grind their
daily grain,
man's wheel of life around
fire, sun and
seasons,
Voar-Simmer-Hairst
to tame the land,
plant-grow-harvest
before black
leanness
of
winter.
Around
this lush realm for mortals,
they build their ting
and chamber
cairns,
harvest from the sea & the land –
scrutinise waves & horizon from
basalt edges of
old rocks,
share
their home with
wandering dead in between
stars & Northern lights.

On either side of
dry stone wall,
tun and scattald
feel a safe
world:

a
place to be born & to die,
raise your offspring with each harvest,
write your story on
every stone –
that perfect realm
you can call
"home".

A Little Chaos

Hands inside gloves,
she prunes and
slashes
through
branches

to find order
within her heart –
she sees chaos among
bluebells & lavender,
lost motherhood,
unfinished
plans;
she
shapes
her world with
a sickle,
fashions
landscapes
inside her shed as
rain runs
cold...
And

as her
sanctuary grows
wild or inside
pots,
she looks & dreams,
there is a light for each flower in the garden.

The Cherry Trees

There, at the foot of a mountain in azure sky,
orchards of dreams in rows of threes,
trees dressed in white –

cherry blossoms,
immaculate

fragrance of spring, fragile,
so faint, awakes senses in honeybees,
like courtesans in a ballroom;

flowers of life, so
delicate.

Bobbing branches in April wind,
like whimsical ballerinas,
I feel humble to your sadness, time in garden that is not
mine;

petals of love in
minuet.

Geopoetics from Provence

1

Open Window

Behind dawn streaks of blue & pink,
   almond green shutters held open, I hear the world,
rattling calls, exotic bird conversations, their furtive
wings between
      fruit trees, naked vines & Provençal tiles...
They tell me so many stories, dawn chorus
perched at heart level -
so melodious, pure as love songs & cherry trees
inside a wind they call "Mistral".

2.

Lumière (Light)

Eight years needed to reconvene with that azure type of
blue.
Peach, almond, apricot blossoms,
and at the beginning of
spring,
I salute your
white
sakura.

The Planets

Princess' den,
adorned with lights after sunset,
 her universe shared for a guest,
there's a fiddle to please Elgar,
a ukulele inside its
case
Each planet,
star, glows on the wall, as
eyes meet dreams -
inside her
heart
so much kindness,
 inside her world,
  there is
   music.

Blue (Rune Poem)

Isa,
rune of ice,
written as I,
in prey to time, there,
motionless;
found in blue boreal forest,
rooted inside depth of winter,
where frost records
prints of our souls in icicles.
As you descend into
our world,
trees bear homage to
your static sense of ego –
they may recite those words for
snow, so many eyes
deep in cold air,
born of lone
clouds in
a blind
sky.
That woman's voice in
the forest, with
a piano,
calls
for
her child
somebody
turn in a snowflake.

Tale from the Blade

"Jesus!" exclaimed Lorna as she stopped still at the Market Cross. Commercial Street was virtually deserted, though filled with fog & greasy smell of deep-fried chips. What was unfolding before her defied the laws of peacefulness at such hour. Not enough beer was yet lashing down Lerwegians' throats at 6 p.m. ... Before her eyes two silhouettes were engaging into brawl. She held her breath.

"Oh Magnus, for da love o God!" she yelled at one whom she suddenly recognised.

Magnus did not answer. In his anger he pulled a knife – that very same knife, shiny-sharp blade he was using at his workplace just alongside the Esplanade. This time Magnus wouldn't fillet a lemon sole or gut herring. He was desperate.

"Dunna... Dunna touch him wi da knife" begged Lorna.

Lorna was barely 17 with a temper so mercurial. "Headstrong" could be her middle name. She was selling the fish Magnus prepared in the backroom at Mr Fraser's shop. Lorna moved without thinking. She leapt towards Magnus like a lion onto an armoured gladiator. Tears were too late. The street's flagstones turned spotted red as soon as steel finished its job. Lorna's brown eyes stared at Magnus; her hands clutching at his shoulders that held all his teenage madness in a moment of delusion. Lorna collapsed into his arms; Magnus stood still like a statue.

"Whit is du done?" suddenly screamed his opponent.

"Dunna touch her, shö is my lass!" Magnus unleashed in sheer terror.

Icelandic Dream

20 more North out of long plume.

Fire dreaming under thick ice,
where arctic fox sleeps on warm flanks of igneous rock,
petrified trolls -
and ptarmigans fake icicles as
camouflage.
So much rhythm, dynamic
names:
Hekla,
  Vatnajökull,
   Kirkjufell,
home of fire,
the unpronounceable great one,
    where men walk alone inside ash; and wild ponies
trek through
heather, tormentil, streams.
Some say your heart came out of hell,
molten-magic-metamorphic,
split wide open, nordic cradle of all our *tings,* where
free men met and ruled their world.
I'm still dreaming of
your Highlands,
harlequin ducks & gyrfalcons;
I've yet to set foot on
your shore.

"Meaning of north"

Seasons

"I listened, waiting for the silence, and heard instead,
A sky full of voices "

K. Steven
(Listening)

Shinto

Each morning feels animistic.

Way of the gods,
       water, rock, sun, sound of silence,
        where water takes its purest form –
I brave the wind
and imagine cherry blossoms paving my way to the bus stop,
temple of tin & Plexiglas always open on my roadside,
where I can shelter from rain, snow,
sleek arctic air, water spirits
destined to die on my shoulders
       or sacrifice themselves to salt...
And if I look in the distance, between tarmac & the ocean,
Watatsumi, blue dragon-god, rises again,
its orange eyes locked inside dawn –
inside my skin tinned sanctuary,
I dedicate a final dream to Toyoukeno ?kami,
Great Spirit of food Abundance,
Izigami no Mikoto,
the Provider of the Five Grains
shint? silence,
      simplicity,
         and ride the dragon
            through the land.

Song of Starlings

Starlings talk like Bushmen;
   listen for their clicks in their song,
            there's Kalahari in Shetland,
      their V-shaped wings glide in day sky,
         glittered feathers touch down on snow.

Thin bills poke through dry bread slices -
they waste no time picking cold crumbs! Through this
winter, can't let
      the starve, my heart is glued to the window.
                  I've nailed apples on all fence posts -
      my eyes check dykes and chimney pots; along with
                  few angry sparrows,
                        they come to
                              feed
                        between
                        blizzards.

Spring's
still hiding under ice;
I hear them sing – they come and go...
      Thin apple cores freeze in the wind; I count their
                  prints left in the snow.

         Will they survive the next morning?
I'll wait for them each new morrow.

Hit Sky

tchack-a-tchack-a-tchack-a-tchack-a-tchack

ice
on metal
—

February
sky like a shooting
Kalashnikov,

fires hail stones on my
car roof just like bullets
on a tin can,

I felt the last round
from the clouds.

87

Spring Light on Bressay

Sign,
signal,
beam of change,
as if low cloud lost a battle,
grey of the ghost looks so aghast,
it's got to shift, shoooooo through the shaft –
shackled to the ship of winter...
Shambolic as rollers & tides,
tired of lingering so long onto our hills & TV masts,
anointing every call of shalders, sleeping petals inside sepals.

Bio-rhythm in equinox,
as sun & moon rock onto scales,
through my window on the fourth floor,
I imagine earthly contours, familiar shapes freed from sky lace
and feel water filling our Sound, pull of our faithful satellite –
blue over washing bridal dress,
fresh epidermis of her skin,
eager to unveil to a sun her every charm
through sighs & dreams.

There,
on the wings of each black back,
it is written.

Welcome to My Life!

1 Sunday Morning in Bridge End
Gok-Gok!
Late Sunday morning in Bridge End.
Come say hello to mister gull,
        cat's eyes level,
like a Buddha,
feline's watching those printed feathers in the sky.
Our souls wander on sleek floor boards;
there's a banjo tied to a voice,
morning slips away with grey clouds,
just like that friendly herring gull
gliding slowly towards Papil.
You're calibrating your
own words –
I'm still sleepy,
my tea's gone cold –
moi, le matin, j'existe pas.

2.Treasure Hunters, Bruck Gatherers
You said April was like a jinx
stuck between hail & the ocean;

so we wandered through ice & wind
towards sandstone
where water brinks
and rewinds life in slow motion.

You hopped and checked a few rock pools
in hope to flag up a starfish;

I stood solemn
to wrecking waves like a vigil,
a memorial riveted to grass & cliff edge
away from their rolling skirmish.

We found our loot among life's junk
so sound asleep there on this shore...
Chinese pictograms on fabric –
weird iron frame,
rust turns to gold between your hands.

3. Your Totem Soul

Here comes that woman
from driftwood –
Luckyminney awaits you home,

like a mother
on her lone shelf,
in Shetland-style that is her own –

stripy long johns,
blue boiler suit,
cosy knickers
(black, size XL!)

"Tea, tattie scones and Jaffa cakes"
her stone table was meant to crack...

Her presence is your totem soul,
a cup of love on this island.

Simmer Dim

we have aligned to sun & moon,
what does it mean to
the shalder?

bright calishang,
cockiloorie instead of ice,
linties & whaap,
feverish song of the blackbird,
wings slashing through a lavish sky,

patchworks of
matrimonial cotton grass
where men and birds share same hillsides, where
peat turns into pyramids.
ever ending,
over-saturated sense of life –
flick of feathers, twisting below this industrious
horizon,

fishermen, birds, as if tradition never dies...

that perpetual canvas of blue in defiance to hands
of time,
like a gigantic bonfire,

we look through the eye of the sun.

Tale from the Sun

Listen to our echoing stars,
another summer goes to bed –
love fades slowly behind sunset,
fire-crimson thicken our sky;
a good night kiss blown by July,
eiders whisper a lullaby;
slipping way in
our pocket.

Feel the retreat of
our burning celestial star,
summer's yawning wrapped in low clouds –
a king-size quilt stuffed to endure
shivering nights;

Dressing August with a dark plaid –
with cosmic lights, God's many eyes, and
silver clock sometimes unplugged,
he won't be disturbed by
her grace & her drifting aero-friends...

Mais l'écho des étoiles on ne l'entend jamais...

Behind thin mist, September wakes –
we'll dress our skin with threads
of wool and kiss
those cold lips of darkness.

Horizons

I watch this sky,
another
cold,
oppressive,
broken -
lost in long
corridors of clouds;
haunting,
daunting,
through
hissing wind.

I steer my
eyes out towards sea
to anchor them
on a beacon -
tallest of cliffs,
triangular,
defiant
in geometry,
on a tight rope,
this thin blue line that
divides us,
you, in heaven,
me,
below clouds
    between now and
        eternity.

Another look,

  line...

My soul disturbed
 by a Merlin
  at eye
 level;
 gangs of
 starlings
 flushed in a flash -
I fear their fear,
 hunted,
  daunted by
 claws & wings
 that will not crash (!)

My horizon blinded by mist,
I sit alone on this
  I drink the
 tears of those
  starlings,
 wandering ghosts
 tied to the
wind,
 aggressive
    sky.

"Last of the Harvest"

Talking Clocks

We're in winter,
the light has gone -
we squabble for scraps like starlings at the foot of the
nearest leaves...

We're in winter,
gales bite our tongues, *skelp wis laek bairns,* in every
corner of lone cliffs,
in every meaning of the ledge...

We're in winter,
rollers chisel through sand & shells like a steam train at
Ninian Sands.

We're in winter,
birds have spoken, flown anywhere for survival, summer
deserted the island -
now new visitors round the loch, from other Nordic edge
of north...

We're in winter,
clocks have spoken, sharpened blades of sharp nights to
come, as
your feet slide back in sheepskin, to shy away from edge
of
the folded metal.

We're in winter,
let's feast on light's final hours,
                    October's gone.

95

Triptych of Halloween Haiku

Moon in eclipse,

may the dead rise among black cats -

boo!

On the last day of October

pumpkin faces on window sills

fog & fright.

Trick or treat,

Pyramids of Quality Street -

Hallowmas at Tesco's.

The Curse of the Full Moon

You stopped to photograph beauty.

What was between North Sea and stars?

Bewitched by her power to shine inside that great indigo room where eyes reflect on horizon, you cried for light instead of wolves and bowed to the great Hunter's Moon.

Who wants to flirt with her dark side?

Crystallised air, night turned to knives. As you decided to go home, car ignition remained silent. You turned the key so many times, that sudden fear steamed up windows...

Your dashboard's jinxed, as it flicked & blinked inside black.

Why do you believe in angels?

You watched headlights whiz on main road. Nobody saw you from above., too busy, focused on cat's eyes... Knives turned to swords. Hunter's Moon beamed indifferent. A seagull's wings across the sea. One simple call, they always come to the rescue.

Pumpkin Juice

To hell with chimes, mice and midnight!
Take a wild ride among dark woods -
two headressed horses
with dark plumes,
ghastly galore,
monochrome
blue
as
night
shines through
shivering leaves...
that slight grin carved to kiss your fears,
that hollow face lit with a match.
Now children left for
trick-or-treat,
let's laugh in the pulp of horror,
distorted void in the mirror,
disturbing flick,
flickering
shadows on slashed walls,
eyes in the earth – furrowing claws – squeeze the
marrowbone off the blade...
Hold your horses:
you dance with ghouls but despise gore -
let's add garlic to pumpkin juice, sieve the concoction
from its seeds, and serve it with dandelion...

Now raise your glass to Hallowmas.

Troswick Scarecrow

Friend of ravens,
         guardian of hay,
look at yourself:
your hat is soaked –
     you don't even scare those starlings
          that come to perch
     on your elbow.

Rain washed & kneeled,
lost in your thoughts,
     blue oil skin,
          you seem to pray,
     breathless,
  broken,
for all your sins & redemption.

          The bogyman rots on its feet,
     too many wings teased
your shadow.

Ferocious Wind

Son of Aeolus & the sea,
you slap at will faces of time -
to the eyes of wandering clouds, compass and charts.

Unreal or just invisible,
you, poltergeist, so hair raising,
your eyes turn green inside thunder,
my soul adrift.

Fair Isle, Ouessant, Cap Finistère,
Force 9 or less,
you, solitary
seafarer,
whistling one.

Men fear
your unforeseen anger;
your claws emerge out of ocean -
why do you hound us
across Earth,
monsieur
le
vent?

Winter Sunrise

Today Picasso sketched our sky;
he's smudged low clouds
with shades of red -
washed off
the stars
erased light rain;
pencilled our wind,
geese
silhouettes
high above waves -
charcoaled our sun
morning light
grey.

"Blackbirds braving icicles"

Waiting for Snow (in a triptych of tongues)

1.

Waiting for snow,
crystalline sighs symmetrical,
    unique & suited for my sky;
        waiting for whiteness like a child -
a sense of home encrypted inside
icicles...
A suite of stars deep in silence.

2.

Waitin an waitin fur da snaa,
da dryin wind o November, da bittersie,
fann an flukra -
da glerl o ice, haily puckles, da bliind moorie,
half oda winter dön at Yöl...

3.

J'attends la neige,
fine, poudreuse, toute étincelée de diamants -
aux yeux divins d'anges éternels, j'attends son retour sur
ma terre,
manteau d'hermine ou de crin blanc,
elle habillera phares et falaises
pour s'oublier dans
l'océan.
Au dire des étoiles et du vent,
        j'attends la neige comme un enfant.

Waiting for Snow – *(2. & 3. Translated)*

2 (from Shetlan)

Waiting & waiting for the snow,
the good drying wind of November, a freezing day,
snowdrift, gentle falling fat snowflakes -
the glaze of ice, icy pellets, blinding blizzard,
half of winter fallen at Yule...

3.
(from French)

I wait for snow,
fine, powder-like, glittering inside her diamonds -
to the divine eyes of everlasting angels, I wait for her
return on my Earth,
coat of ermine or of white mane,
she will clad all lights and headlands
to lose herself in
the ocean.
To the stars' and the wind's daresay,
I'm waiting for snow like a child.

...Waitin fur da snaa laek a bairn!

Winter Spirit

Today I made my home ready to welcome darkest of
season.

Fruit of the rose in the garden,
    crown of holly in your honour,
        the thinnest moon at its zenith,
icicle sky –

your eyes, those juniper berries,
poured in mulled wine,
    we toast to our despotic star to rise again from its
ashes;

playful Amabael smiles outside.

Runic dream found in Nordic night,
    we shall feast by the bowing spruce, light bonfires on
every hill,
        meddle with creatures of the cairns,
free to wander with the living...

They say it starts on Tulya's E'en.

For you,
dark world, my offerings – cinnamon stick & evergreen,
my wheel of light instead of fears,
my sheaf of corn,
reassurance.

Light Recordings

spring

indigo blue,
interwoven sounds of curlews,
wrens & blackbirds – tap-dancing rain,
snippik drumming beyond midnight;
migrating shalders to Iceland.

summer

boreal-blue, electric white,
sunsets too lazy in sea fog –
redshanks, peewits just won't shut down;
waders return from Arctic.

autumn

dim, honey-gold,
often tormented by the wind –
a million feathers on passage
are hiding low in our heather;
wild geese talk Russian in their sleep...
Early gales whistle their return.

winter
metallic grey, blunt eerie dark,
sometimes draped to elude our eyes –
yellow, red, green,
gift from the sun...
gangs of starlings gather to glow
better on snow, black against white;
10 days of gale
shortened by night
deafen our souls.

"My Nordic world from a window"

Acknowledgements

My grateful thanks for their encouragement and support go to the following:

Alec Cluness & Donald Anderson from Shetland Arts; Laureen Johnson & Brian Smith from The New Shetlander; The Lerwick & Westside Writers' Groups; The Shetland Library; NorthWords Now; Suckingmud; Poetry Scotland (Open Mouse); Norman Bissell from the Scottish Centre for Geopoetics; Shetland's former Writers-in-Residence, Raman Mundair, Jen Hadfield and Kevin MacNeil for casting their respective critical eye over *Compass Head;* to Edwin Morgan, Christine De Luca, Jen Hadfield and Kenneth Steven for opening each book section, to Monica Hansebakken for her staves, and to Nordland Publishing for opening their home in the snow.

La Presse à pommes/The Apple Press & *Dis Midder Tongue* were first published in the New Shetlander (Simmer Issue 2004); *My Great Grand Mother's Hands*, first published in the New Shetlander, (Voar Issue 2007); *Errances/Wanderings* first published in Stravaig (Scottish Centre for Geopoetics online journal); *Confession to a* Foreigner was first published in Poetry Scotland's Open Mouse; A *Tale of Two Harbours* & *Horizons* both first published in NorthWords Now (Nov 2006); *Shipwright* first appeared in Wastside Noir (Sep.2015);*The Samurai* was first published in the Launch Issue of suckingmud (Feb 2007); *Northern Roost* first published in NorthWords Now (Spring 2006).

About the Author

Nat Hall is a Norman born, Shetland-based poet & visual artist, educated on French & British shores, Aix-en-Provence & Oxford. She is a member of Shetland Arts' Writers Groups, Shetland ForWirds, The Federation of Writers (Scotland), ArtiPeeps (England), The Humblyband Crew (Ruth Macdougall's Humblyband Project, Scotland), The Scottish Centre for Geopoetics, under the directorship of Norman Bissell (Scotland) & the World Poetry Movement (global). She contributed to the Canadian Poetry Association, as a "world poet" as well as an Assistant Editor/Consultant for *Poemata* at River Bones Press, Moncton, NB (2008-10). Selected works featured in *anthologies, The Pull Of The Moon or Bicycle Dreams, Shetland New Writing Anthology,* [ISBN – 0904562751] [Scotland, 2004], *Pushing Out The Boat, Issue 10* [ISBN 1471 – 8502], [Scotland, 2010], *& The Al Purdy A-Frame Anthology,* collaborative writing with D. Allard - *[ISBN 13: 978-1-55017-502-8 ISBN 10: 1-55017-502-5], Canada, (2009); co-authored From Shore to Shoormal / D'un rivage à l'autre* with Donna Allard [BJP, Canada, 2012]; *and in other literary places - Shetland Life, the New Shetlander, NorthWords Now, Bright Pebbles* (Photography), [ISBN 978-0-905924-87-8], Scotland (2010)*, The Poetry of Scotland, Poésie française, suckingmud, Poetry Scotland - The Battered Suitcase, Cella Round Trip [USA], and Poemata, Canada.*

Blog & Website at:

https://nordicblackbird.wordpress.com/
http://www.nordicblackbird.weebly.com/

Glossary of Shetland dialect/Scots words

bairn – a child / *skelp wis laek bairns* – slap us like children

boannie – nice, lovely

bonxie – great skua

bruck – rubbish

calishang – boystrous noises

cockiloorie - daisy

craigs – the first rocks nearest to the shore.

dee (laek dee) – you (like you)

dunna - don't

Hairst – seaon of havest (Autumn)

hame - home

humli-baand – the piece of rope that ties the oar to the "kabe".

kabe - piece of wood/metal that keeps the oar in place.

linties an whaap – twites and curlew

Midder tongue – mother tongue, language of birth.

Muckle Flugga – the most northerly point of Shetland, where the last lighthouse stands.

ness – headland

Peewits – *A northern lapwing*

The Roost – the tidal race at the tip of Sumburgh Head, where the North Sea and Atlantic meet.

scattald – area of common grazing

shalders – oystercatchers

selkies – seals

shoormal – the shallows, area of the sea, where rollers shift sand.

Shö - she

Simmer – summer; *Simmer Dim*: very light night, nightless in summer.

skerries – small rocky islands

solan - gannet

Sooth moother – incomer (via the South Mouth of the Bressay Sound in Lerwick)

Sound – an open stretch of sea between islands

stravaig – wander

tirricks – arctic terns

ting – (from O.N.) a place of (Viking) parliament

Tulya's E'en – in the old calandar, the start of Yule celebration, one night seven days before Yule day, known as "The Dead Return".

tun - township

tushkar – the tradition tool to cut peat

tysties – black guillemots

Voar – Spring, season of planting.

wirds – words

"Whit is du done?" - "what have you done?"

yarn – to talk, speak

NORDLAND PUBLISHING

Follow the North Road.

nordlandpublishing.com
facebook.com/nordlandpublishing
nordlandpublishing.tumblr.com

www.nordlandpublishing.com

Printed in Great Britain
by Amazon

24555286R00072